Jacques and Gilles in the New World

The Ancestors of the Lozons of Michigan

By

Sandi McIntyre and Doris Lozon

ISBN# 978-1-304-62142-9

Printed in U.S.A.

This book is dedicated to all of the descendants of Gilles Lauzon and Jacques Archambault, and all of the adventurers in our great family: To those who are willing to move overseas; to those who take up challenging pursuits; to those who reach out to help others; to those who are willing to change vocations mid-life; to those unafraid of the unknown.

I hope this little book can explain why we are, the way we are. And I hope we never change!

Lauzon Family Crest

Once upon a time...

Gilles Lauzon was born in 1631 to Pierre and Anne (nee Boivin) Lauzon (he was born in 1600, she in 1604) in the parish of St. Julien in Caen, Normandy. Gilles was an only child—very unusual in a Catholic family. Maybe he wasn't the only child born; rather, the sole surviving child. He was apprenticed to a local smith, and quickly became a talented copper-and-tinsmith.

In those days, a youngster who wanted to become a smith was generally apprenticed to a master smith for 4 – 6 years (unpaid). During this time, they would learn how to make pill boxes, cookie cutters, and other simple items. Later, they would learn how to make more complex items, such as cake and pie pans, milk pails, and basins. Last, they would learn how to fabricate complicated pieces such as chandeliers and crooked-spout coffee pots. After the apprenticeship was completed, the young smith became a journeyman, not yet being a master smith who would employ others (or take on an apprentice). Many young smiths took to the road as peddlers or tinkers, in an effort to save enough money to open a shop in town.

Gilles was 22 years old, and already a *Maitre-Chaudronnier,* or Master Coppersmith, when he was recruited in 1653 by Paul Chomeday de Maisoneuve, the founder of Ville-Marie (a new settlement in New France). Chomeday hoped to cash in on the wealth of furs, primarily beaver, available in the area, partially for his beloved France, and partially for his own selfish financial interests.

Ville-Marie was, at the time, the western-most French settlement in all of New France. It was founded in 1642 as part of a project to further the French colonial empire. In time, it would come to be called Montreal.

France's first attempt to settle their new territory was to send in *Compagnie de Cent-Associes* (Company of One Hundred Associates).

But by 1651, Ville-Marie was reduced to 50 residents. The Mohawk and Iroquois Indians were showing no mercy. Chomeday needed 100 men to protect the border of the town from attacking Iroquois Indians. He had decided that, if he wasn't able to recruit enough men, that he would abandon Ville-Marie, and move everyone back down the river to Quebec.

The men were recruited primarily from the French areas Picardie, Champagne, Ile-de-France, Normandy, Anjou, and Maine. Why primarily these areas? Because there were no newspapers (and most people were illiterate anyways), the only way the French government had to get information out was through the local churches and clergy. Folks who lived too far out in the country didn't have access to very much information.

The question is why did Gilles enlist? As an only son, he would have inherited all of his father's assets. Perhaps he didn't get along with his father, or maybe he was very patriotic or restless. Or maybe he wanted to explore the world and see what else was out there.

As a member of *"le Grande Recrue"* (The Great Recruit), he, along with 121 other men, enlisted with the *Compagnie de Montreal* (Montreal Company). Their purpose was to populate and tame the colony of New France. Trapping beaver furs was the primary occupation, but support personnel were needed to make the copper-ware, provide livestock for food and transportation, and grow crops. The trappers also needed a somewhat safe environment, free from hostile natives. The men recruited were a mix of soldiers, farmers, and craftsmen, with a few officers thrown in for good measure.

All recruits were committed for five years, at a rate of 80 livres (one livre was equal to one pound of silver, and was subdivided into 20 sols or 12 deniers) in salary per year. Gilles received an advance of 127 livres, 7 sols, and 10 deniers on the day he embarked. In today's (2013) money, he was contracted to earn $28,787 USD per year, and received an advance of $46,071 USD.

France

The ship that the recruits were to sail to Montreal on was the *Saint-Nicolas de Nantes*, under the command of Captain Pierre le Besson, was in rather poor condition. After sailing 350 miles out to sea, the un-seaworthy vessel was forced by leaks to turn back. Water seeping into the holds threatened to spoil all the provisions. Sister Marguerite Bourgeoys, who was aboard to serve Ville Marie as a school teacher, wrote that she was afraid that they were all going to perish without benefit of a priest on board.

The passengers were dropped off on an island before the ship docked at Saint Nazaire. The reason for this was that Chomeday was worried that after the short but frightening sea voyage, some of the recruits may slip away and return home. Being stranded on an island, they were prevented from doing so. Another ship was found, the *Sainte-Marguerite*. The baggage and supplies reloaded, the spoiled supplies replaced, and passengers re-boarded. All this was done at the expense of the Compagnie de Montreal. They set sail on July 20, and landed at Quebec on September 22, 1653. Eight of the passengers died at sea due to sickness, but our Gilles Lauzon arrived safely.

The ship landed at Quebec after a voyage of 64 days. Governor de Lauzon (not related—in fact, his family line died out) refused to let the men have the boats they needed to finish the trek to Montreal, as they were sorely needed for the defense of Quebec. Gilles and the rest of the recruits finally arrived in Ville-Marie on November 16, after trekking overland for almost two months and a distance of at least 150 miles. Their numbers had dropped, and would drop even more.

Of the approximately 150 men who signed on in France, only 95 arrived in Ville-

Marie. Of the 95, 24 died at the hands of the Iroquois, four drowned, and one man died when his house caught fire. Several others who made the voyage with Gilles also joined our family tree.

Having been in Montreal only three months, Gilles agreed on February 15, 1654, to reside at Ville-Marie permanently, and received a bonus of 500 livres ($180,000 USD in 2013 currency). He evidently had no longing for his homeland, and chose to make his future in the New World.

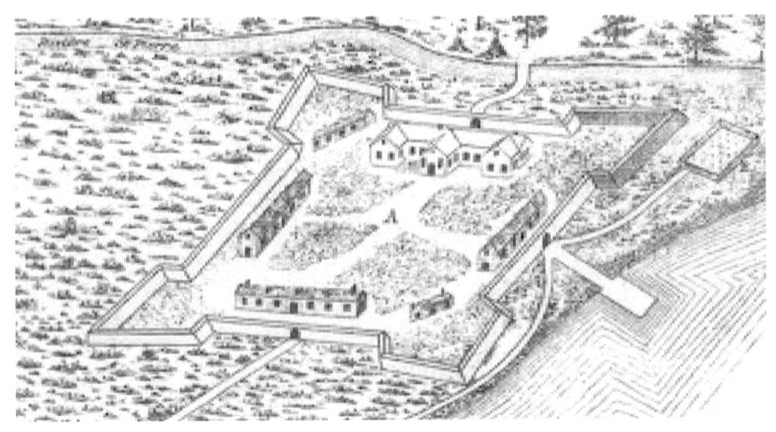

The fort at Montreal

Now Gilles could afford to buy some land. In 1655, Chomeday deeded to Gilles 30 arpents--approximately 25 acres--of land within the town, in gratitude for his service. A few months later, Gilles entered an agreement to purchase a piece of land which was 50 perches square--approximately 15-1/2 acres—upon which sat a house, for the price of 330 livres. The note was paid in full within twenty months.

With housing taken care of, Gilles' thoughts turned to love. The girl he loved was Marie Archambault, although she was still quite young. The youngest of her family, she was called Marie-Louise, and confusingly enough, was the second "Marie" her father sired—the first married Urbain Tessier.

Her father was a comrade of Gilles'. Jacques Archambault had arrived in Ville Marie in 1645 or 1646 as a member of

Compagnie de Cent-Associes. He is perhaps best known for sinking the first water-well

Jacques Archambault

Archambault Family Crest

inside the fort at Montreal, done at the request of Chomeday. There are at least two plaques in Montreal commemorating the well. It was a very important task, because with the new well, the colonists would have an ample supply of water during Indian sieges—of which there were many. Jacques engineered several more wells in the area in years to come. As he had been a vintner in his native France, the New World was offering a whole new set of challenges.

A couple of side-notes: Jacques and his immediate family are the only known Archambaults who have immigrated to the New World from France—so if you know anybody by that name, they are distant relatives! And it is commonly believed that the family has French royalty in their pre-Jacques history, but it remains unproven.

Three years after Jacques' first wife (Marie's mother) passed away, he married again, to Marie Denot de la Martiniere. She was the widow of Mathieu Labat, whose descendants founded the famous Labatt brewery.

A plaque commemorating Jacques Archambault's first well on the island of Montreal. The translation reads *"Near this place, JACQUES ARCHAMBAULT (1604-1688), ancestor of all American Archambaults, dug the first well in 1658 on the island at the request of Governor Maisonneuve."*

This plaque hangs on the Church Dompierre-sur-Mer, in Archambault's home town of Dompierre-sur-Mer, France. Translated, it reads, *"1604 LE DOMPIERROIS 1688 JACQUES ARCHAMBAULT, Sole ancestor of the American Archambaults, was baptized in this church. His descendants are grateful. JACQUES ARCHAMBAULT OF AMERICA. 31 MAY 1988."*

So we can see that Jacques was at least as important in Montreal as Gilles Lauzon was—perhaps even more so. And both of these amazing men are our first North American ancestors!

Gilles and Marie were wed November 27, 1656 in Montreal. He was 25 years old; she was twelve.

Unknown to Gilles, his mother passed away in France on his wedding day.

The first baby was a girl, Michelle, born September 1657, at their home in Montreal. The following month, the first school in the area was opened in an old stable. At least Gilles' children would have access to an education—a benefit he'd never had. In 1658, Gilles sold the house and land parcel. Perhaps the new wife didn't care for it. In any event, it was purchased by Jean Chaperon, for the price of 800 livres. He would have made a tidy profit of 470 livres on that sale! But Chaperon backed out of the deal four months later. Four months later, Gilles traded the same house and land for another owned by Jean Auger, who promised to pay 375 livres to make up the difference. Six days later, Auger resold this property for 600 livres to Jean Gasteau, who, on the same day, unloaded it onto Jacques Milot for 700 livres. Pierre Lorrain became its owner on August 6, 1659, for the price of 900 livres. Also in the same year, Pierre Ducharme bought Gilles' other 25 acres of land, which now boasted a house. Our ancestor was now cash-rich but land-poor. The family most likely lived above the smithy until a new piece of land was purchased.

Shortly before this convoluted real estate deal concluded, the family was increased again. Marguerite was born 20 months after Michelle, and their mother must have been chronically exhausted!

Gilles was ready to become a landowner again by August 1661, when he leased 40 arpents (34 acres) from Pierre Bessonnette. This land was located on the Saint-Louis hill. In December 1662, a contract to purchase was signed. Gilles had been in New France less than ten years, and he was a husband, father, land owner, and the only Master-copper-and-tinsmith in town.

Whatever the reasons that caused him to leave his homeland, Gilles was on his way to becoming a wealthy and successful man.

Baby number three arrived around this time. Francoise made her appearance in 1662, followed 19 months later by the fourth daughter, Marie, in 1663. Mother Marie must have put her foot down, because there were no more children born until 1666, when yet another girl, Catherine joined the family.

The little town of Ville-Marie was an easy target for marauding Iroquois, for even in the dead of winter, they could lead a deadly and effective attack against the small town. February 1662 saw no fewer than 200 natives launching an attack, leaving four French dead and eight hostages. In response, the governor of Montreal established the *Milice de la Sainte-Famille de Jesus, Marie and Joseph* (Militia of the Holy Family of Jesus, Mary and Joseph). In January 1663, men were signing up. The unpaid volunteers were organized into 20 squads, each with a corporal and six militia men. Gilles Lauzon joined as the first militia man of the 14th squad under Corporal Louis Artus de Sailly. Jacques Archambault was also a member.

During this period of increased Indian hostilities, out-laying families were requested, for their own safety, to move within the walls of the fort.

Nobody will ever know how many days and nights Gilles and Jacques were on sentry duty, or how much fighting they were involved in. They did their duty, and helped protect the fort and their families.

The King of France realized soon after that his Company of One Hundred Associates was too small for the mission he had set before them. The Montreal Company resigned control, and the Crown took over governorship of New France. A Governor General and an Intendant were appointed, a Sovereign Council was established, and in 1665, the Carignan

Regiment was sent. The Carignan Regiment was an infantry unit, and required seven ships to transport men and equipment across the Atlantic Ocean. All residents of little Ville-Marie were happy with the changes, and slept better at night. Soon, the farmers were able to move back to their homesteads.

A census was conducted in New France in 1666 and 1667. Records show that 35 year old tinsmith Gilles Lauzon and his 22 year old wife had five children, eight head of cattle, and 40 arpents of land under cultivation. The household also claimed two domestic servants, most likely to work the land while Gilles was busy making pots, pans, buckles, and hardware for the community. He was likely also responsible for any blacksmithing work at the fort – shoeing the horses, and making iron works. Any welders in our family can probably thank him for their genes!

Gilles Lauzon, Master Coppersmith

Seraphin arrived into the Lauzon family in 1668. Gilles finally had a son! His eldest daughter Michelle married Jean Coron in 1670. Daughter number six Louise was born in 1671 and daughter number two Marguerite married in 1672. Michel arrived in 1673. Francoise married the next year, and Paul was born in 1675. Three more girls were born—Marie Madeleine born in 1677; then Anne and Jeanne, who passed away at the ages of two and five respectively. Marie married in 1680, and Catherine doing the same the following year. Eldest daughter Michelle died in 1683, and Gilles Jr. was born in 1684. Tragically, the mother of all of these children died at the age of 41, when the boy was only a little more than one year old. Between baptisms and burials, this family knew how the keep the local clergy busy!

In 1678, Jacques Archambault's sons petitioned the Governor for a government pension for their old father, as he was no longer able to farm, or do any productive work. The Governor allowed the pension, and Jacques lived comfortably another ten years, until his death at age 84.

Gilles didn't re-marry after the passing of his wife, as was common in those days. A man had to have help raising his family. That he never re-married may be a testament to how much in love he was with his young bride. Maybe he hired a nanny for his 11 surviving children. Or, maybe he just didn't have time -- Gilles passed away September 21, 1687, only two years later. Seraphin was 19 years old, but somebody had to take care of Michel (age 11), Paul (age 9), Marie Madeleine (age 7), and Gilles Jr (age 1). Presumably the older children helped raise the younger ones.

Gilles Lauzon

Family lore says that our first ancestor in the New World was hung as a horse thief, but that is very unlikely. Gilles had enough wealth to be comfortable, and could even afford servants. There is no reason to believe he had fallen so low as to steal a horse. In fact, there is no record that I can find anywhere that shows any of our ancestors being jailed (until recent generations!) or executed. This is just a piece of romantic family lore.

There was, however, a Michael Lauzon who was executed in Montreal sometime after 1764. He was not one of ours. There were three unrelated Lauzons who emigrated to New France. One is Gilles, our line; one was the line of the Governor, which later died out; and the third line – the prisoner's line.

During the autumn in which Gilles died, the town of Ville-Marie was ravaged by an outbreak of typhus (not to be confused with typhoid), which killed nearly ten percent of the white settlers. I think it is very likely that our first North American ancestor died more in need of antibiotics than a horse.

Jacques Archambault died in February, five months after Gilles. It is possible he died of typhus also.

As the men were taming the wilderness and the local Indians, they didn't forget the joys of women. Many took Indian squaws as wives. The Catholic Church did not approve of that practice at all. These white men needed to have white wives, the Church believed. But where were they going to come from? There were only three ways for a young woman to come to New France—with her father (as Marie Archambault did); paying her own passage; or by becoming an indentured servant for three years to one of the wealthy men of New France. Some made their own way across the water, but not nearly enough.

The King of France solved the problem of the lack of white women by offering to pay the dowry of any woman who wanted to help settle France's new holding. If a woman didn't have a dowry, her marriage prospects—and financial future—was quite bleak. One couldn't even join a convent without a dowry! Girls who had lost one or both parents were very vulnerable. There were many of these women with no dowry who welcomed the chance to marry, even if it meant going to the untamed wilderness.

Around 800 of these women accepted the King's offer. They came to be known as *les filles du roi*, or The King's Daughters. The dowry provided 50 livres if the woman married a soldier or 100 livres if she married an officer. In addition, the dowry included:

> *1 head dress, 1 taffeta handkerchief, 1 pair of shoe ribbons, 100 sewing needles, 1 comb, 1 spool of white thread, 1 pair of stockings, 1 pair of gloves, 1 pair of scissors. 2 knives, 1000 pins, 1 bonnet, 4 lace braids, and 2 livres in silver money.*

Upon arrival in New France, the Sovereign Council provided some suitable clothing, as well as food provisions from the king's warehouse.

When a match was made (and many of these women married within two weeks of landing in New France!), the newly married couple was given 50 livre for provisions, an ox, a cow, two pigs, two chickens, two barrels of salt meat, and 11 crowns (one crown equaled approximately 1/24 of a livre). The men now had very good incentive to marry the imported white women instead of breeding with the local heathens.

We have at least two of these brave, remarkable women as ancestors.

Gilles and Marie's eighth child Michel Lauzon grew up, as children tend to do. He married Marie-Anne Coitou at the relatively old age of 29. She was fifteen, born in Quebec. Her mother, Marie-Therese Petit, was a King's Daughter. They married May 15, 1702, in Pointe-aux-Trembles.

Michel apparently did not follow in his father's footsteps and become a coppersmith. He was most likely involved with farming, in order to feed the population at the fort -- an occupation which continued for several more generations.

They had 14 children, with at least five not surviving infancy. These are the surviving children: Francois-Marie was born in 1703, followed by Michael, Madeleine, Marie-Joseph, Marie-Raphael, Marie-Anne in 1704 (Michel and Anne must have loved the name Marie!), Pierre in 1707, Catherine in 1711, and Gabriel, born May 27, 1715.

There is a side-story with this generation. It doesn't tie into us, specifically, but I thought it was interesting.

In the early history of New England and Canada, there was a lot of violence between the French Catholics in Canada and the strict Protestants on New England. Much of it was blamed on the Indians. In other words, the French would get their Indian friends to make raids on New England villages, and the English were doing the same. The Indians were happy just to make mischief; they didn't care much for either group of white folks.

There is some disagreement as to whether Hannah Heard was taken captive in January 1691 or 1692. There were raids on the area near Dover, NH and York, MA, which were only a few miles apart. Hannah had been visiting relatives in York and went for a walk along the river. She was stolen by the Indians, kept for about one year, and eventually taken to Montreal. There, she was adopted (ransomed) by Paul Prudhomme, who was a gunsmith and locksmith. Hannah helped in the family, which already had four children. She was taught as a Catholic, and was baptized as Mary Anne in 1694.

She was named in her father's will, and was to be given money by the executor if she ever returned home. She never returned.

This is a story, which with all the facts makes me want to invent more to the story. Hannah's mother had died, and she had two younger sisters and one younger brother. Her father remarried, and in 1691, the first sister of his second family was born. Since we all know what a girl of ten or eleven years was expected to do in those times, we can assume she was probably little more than a house slave and baby-sitter. Or worse yet, possibly for a step-mother she didn't care for.

The Prudhomme family evidently treated her well, regarding her as a true member of their family. She probably felt she was better off in Canada. One of her grandmothers was described as a 'sober and pious' woman (Hannah's father was Reverend Joseph Hull, an Episcopal

Minister) and the other was the wife of the Governor of New Hampshire. Life in New England was very likely very grim and dutiful; whereas the French in Canada were known for their gaiety and festivals, and a generally light-hearted attitude. We can only guess at what she felt, but when Hannah (Mary Anne) grew up and was able to, she never returned to her family.

There is unproven speculation that Hannah's fathers' family had a bit of royalty in their line.

She married Sebastian Cholet, and raised eleven children with him.

This is how her story ties into our story: One of the children she reared with Sebastian Cholet was named Jacques Cholet. Jacques married Antoinette Amable Legault, and they gave birth to Ursule Cholet. Ursule married Jacques Lauzon, who was the eldest son of Francois-Marie

Lauzon, son of Michel Lauzon. She was what we might call Michel's "grandmother-in-law." But our story follows Gabriel, the youngest in the family...

Up until this time, Montreal had acted as a trans-shipment point to the interior of New France. Ships were unable to travel up the St. Lawrence River past Montreal due to the severe rapids. Goods had to be unloaded and portaged, sometimes warehoused for a length of time. All of this made Montreal a major distribution hub, rather than a one-horse trading post. The larger ships weren't even able to make it to Montreal; they had to unload at Quebec, and send their goods to Montreal on smaller boats. In 1735, a road was finally built, next to the river, for the transport of goods. It was a grand improvement.

The baby of the family, Gabriel, married, at the age of 30, Marie-Anne LaCombe, age 18, from Quebec. Her paternal grandfather, Jean LaCombe, was likely a member of *le Grande Recrue* with Gilles, and her fathers' maternal grandfather (Nicolas Millet) definitely was, as well as her mothers' maternal grandfather. This was definitely a case of many family lines coming together! We have many, many adventurers in our bloodline!

They brought five children into the world—and several of them Maries!—but lost two. Marie-Joseph (named for his sister) died in 1748, in her infancy. Marie-Catherine arrived in 1752, Marie-Anne in 1753, and Pierre-Gabriel was born in 1753 but passed away two years later. Joseph Amable Lauzon joined the family on March 23, 1756, and Marie-Genevieve in 1758. Frontier life was very difficult on everyone, but most especially small children.

Two years later, Ville-Marie was surrendered to the British army, following defeat at the Battle of the Plains of Abraham. And the fur trade carried on, benefitting England now, instead of France. The family was now technically British.

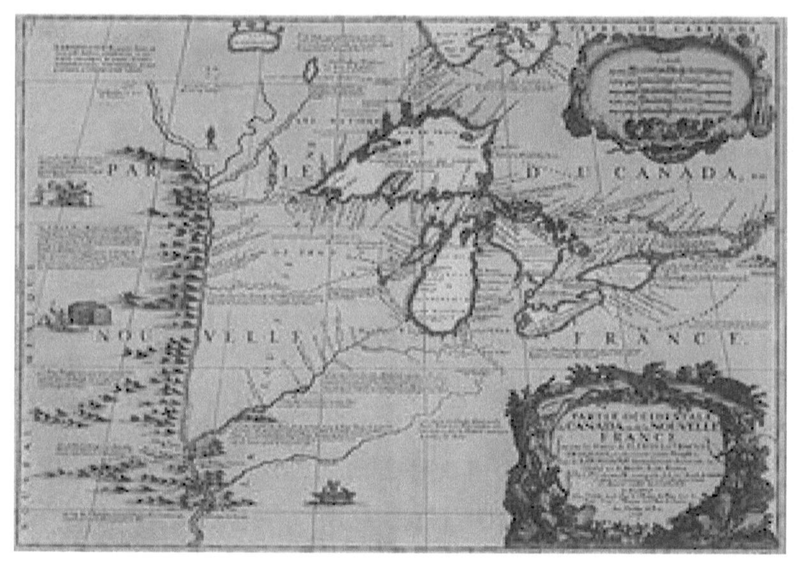

Map of New France, 1688

Joseph Amable Lauzon married Marie Libersan in Montreal in 1780. Marie had two *le Grande Recrue* members and one King's Daughter in her ancestry. One was Antoine Beaudry, her great-great-great grandfather on her father's side; the other was Urbain Jette, her great-great grandfather on her mother's side. The King's Daughter was Catherine Guyard, who was married to Antoine Beaudry. (More adventurers!)

They had three children—Antoine (1793), Josephte (1796), and Michel (1784), named for his great-grandfather.

It is fortunate for us that Joseph Amable bred so productively in his youth, because he never got to see old age. He passed away at the tender age of 29. Both of his daughters perished before reaching adulthood, so Michel was the only hope of his line continuing. Our family line very nearly died out!

Michel Lauzon married Marguerite Choret in 1805. They brought Augustin, Felix, Isaac, Francis Xavier, Isadore, Adalaide, Marguerite, Marie, and Esther into the world.

Isadore was born in 1811. He married Pelagie Usereau, nine years his junior, in 1837. Their additions to the world population were Denise, Louise-Arvide, Amedee, Isadore Jr, Domitilde, John Baptiste, Marguerite, Marcelle, Napolean (Paul), Arvide, Aglae, and William. Isadore Sr was forced to leave this world before his last child was born, leaving poor Pelagie to raise 12 children on her own.

Paul Lauzon was born in 1852. For six generations, the family hadn't strayed very far from Gilles' old homestead near Montreal, but that was about to change. The beaver were becoming scarce, and the fur trade was dying. Another source of income had to be found.

Word was out in Montreal that good farmland was to be had in Bay County, Michigan, and there were lumbering jobs available, so several of the families made the move. Paul, Isadore Jr and their mother, Pelagie, moved to Kawkawlin in 1872. Most likely, the rest of the family was married and settled elsewhere by this time. Older brother John Baptiste had gone ahead, setting up a farm in Bay County in 1864.

Along with changing nationalities, Paul changed names—Lauzon was now Lozon.

The previous year, Gabriel and Adele (nee Bissonnet) Dore had moved to Michigan from Quebec, along with their parents, probably for the same reasons. They also settled in the Kawkawlin area. They brought their 16 year old daughter

Mary with them. Mary was one of 11 children, three of whom died during infancy. Gabriel Dore apparently died of dysentery at age 65.

Paul and Mary married in 1879, in Kawkawlin. They added to the Lozon tribe Josephine, Archie, Mary Louise, Joseph, Telephore, Oddelia, and Laura. All seven of his children were born in Kawkawlin. The first generation of American Lozons! (And American names! Not a single Marie!)

The soil in Bay County was remarkably fertile, and made wonderful harvests. Sugar beets, corn, dry beans, and wheat grew exceptionally well. Hay and livestock also did well.

The Dore, Bissonnet, and Lozon men all worked their farms in the summer, and likely worked in the lumber camps in the winter.

Widowed and alone, Adele and Pelagie both went to live with Paul and Mary in their later years. When Doris Lozon asked them about it in their later years, both Ed and Ona could remember their grandmothers banging their canes on the floor and scolding the children in French for being too noisy.

This book wouldn't be complete without some information on Alice Traxler's family. Doris wrote up these notes, in preparation for this book:

From information available to me, it would appear that the Traxler brothers, Peter and Michael, left their home in the Palatinate, on the Rhine River in Germany, after the harvest in September 1771. They had been recruited by representatives of the Penn family, a well-to-do English family who were Quakers and who had been granted the area of what is now Pennsylvania by the Crown, under certain conditions. They attempted to get as many Quakers as possible to emigrate and went to Germany and recruited there, as there were many Dunkards and other sects who were much like the Quakers. They wanted to be left in peace and not embroiled in the various wars in which Europe was constantly involved.

The Traxlers were young, probably 21 and 19 (Peter was born in 1750). They went down the Rhine to Rotterdam where they embarked in the ship Tyger, George Johnston, Captain. Anyways, the Traxlers embarked and "stood out" for America. They had to stop at Cowes on the Isle of Wight to get a British clearance (health, suitability and character). They then went on, uneventfully, for eight weeks, landing at Philadelphia, Pennsylvania on November 19th, 1771. When they disembarked they took an oath of loyalty to King George III, then reigning in Great Britain, and to the Proprietors of the province of

Pennsylvania. Being of a religious bent, the oath was binding for life and Peter kept his word.

They had relatives in the persons of Jeremiah and Peter Traxler who had emigrated in 1734, and no doubt, that is where they first headed. Peter Jr is our ancestor and it appears that he married about 1777 and lived in the province of New Jersey.

The Traxlers were illiterate. When the war for Independence broke out, there was no doubt as to where Peter's loyalty lay; he soon signed up with the British forces in Ohio. As he says in his second land application in 1798, he was a loyalist for 26 years.

His brother Michael remained in the states.

After the war, when the new states started prosecuting the Loyalists, Peter moved his family to land on the River Rouge in the Detroit area. Soon that land was given back to the States. By this time he had already been into Ontario and was squatting on land in Kent County, located on the River Thames near Chatham. Two hundred acres was eventually granted to him on his petition, and his grown sons each got the same amount of land. Eventually, he owned 1400 acres in this region. This was sufficient for division among his sons upon his death in 1825.

****

So, to keep the story line straight, here is the list of 'begat's….

Peter Traxler Sr (CA 1750 – 1825) married Barbara (no last name found), and they sired Peter Jr in 1775-8, Michael, Barbara, John, Elizabeth, Susan, and Christian.

Peter Traxler Jr (1775-8 – 1846) married Rebecca Fields and birthed Michael, Magdalene & Peter (twins), John P, Barbara, Susan, Daniel, Margaret, James, and Hannah. (On a side note, Susan Traxler seems to be an ancestor to Doris, who is a Lozon by marriage only).

John P. Traxler (1817 - 1883) married Mary Ann McCubbin, and had Peter, Hannah, Rebecca, Robert, Susan, and Daniel.

Robert Traxler (1844 – 1916) married Margaret Winter, and blessed us with Earlin, Harry, Ethel, George, Robert, and Alice.

And we all know that Alice grew up to marry Archie Lozon, in Kawkawlin, Michigan.

As a side-note, Michigan elected J. Bob Traxler as its 8th District Representative. He served from 1974-1993, and was, of course, a Democrat. He was born in Kawkawlin, Bay County, on July 21, 1931. While he is not an ancestor, he is most certainly a relative.

Young Archie Lozon continued the tradition of farming in Kawkawlin and working in the lumber camps. He married Alice Traxler in 1904. They also had a handful of children—between 1904 and 1910 they bore Edmund Napolean, Ona Marie, Robert Joseph, and Chester James. They were all born in Kawkawlin, but the next baby, Ernie, was born in Prescott, in Ogemaw County.

L-R, back to front: Bob, Spike, Chester, Alice, Archie, Phyllis, and Ona (photo taken while Ernie was at war.)

The family had left Kawkawlin and lived in Prescott because their home had burned to the ground in 1913.

During World War 1, Dow Chemical built a charcoal plant in Grayling, Michigan, and the growing family moved to Grayling. Archie suffered moderately from silicosis the rest of his life. The last two children, Clyde (Spike) and Phyllis, were born in Grayling.

Archie Lozon

The first part of the home farm in Maple Forest Township that Archie bought was 40 acres, purchased on Land Contract in late 1919 from Frank Goblet. The purchase price of $1000 was to be paid $100 per year for 10 years. There was no house on this land, so they continued living in their Grayling home.

In 1921, Paul Lozon purchased the old Lozon homestead we all remember, on Hartwick Pines Road. He bought it from Arnold and Gladys Johnson, and paid $600. Upon his death, the land was transferred to Archie and Alice.

Times were hard, even during the "Roaring Twenties". It didn't help at all that the house burned in the winter of 1923-4. Ernie Lozon recalled that he and his siblings were housed all over Maple Forest Township. While the ground was still frozen, fires were started to thaw the ground enough to lay a new foundation. This family was not very happy being apart.

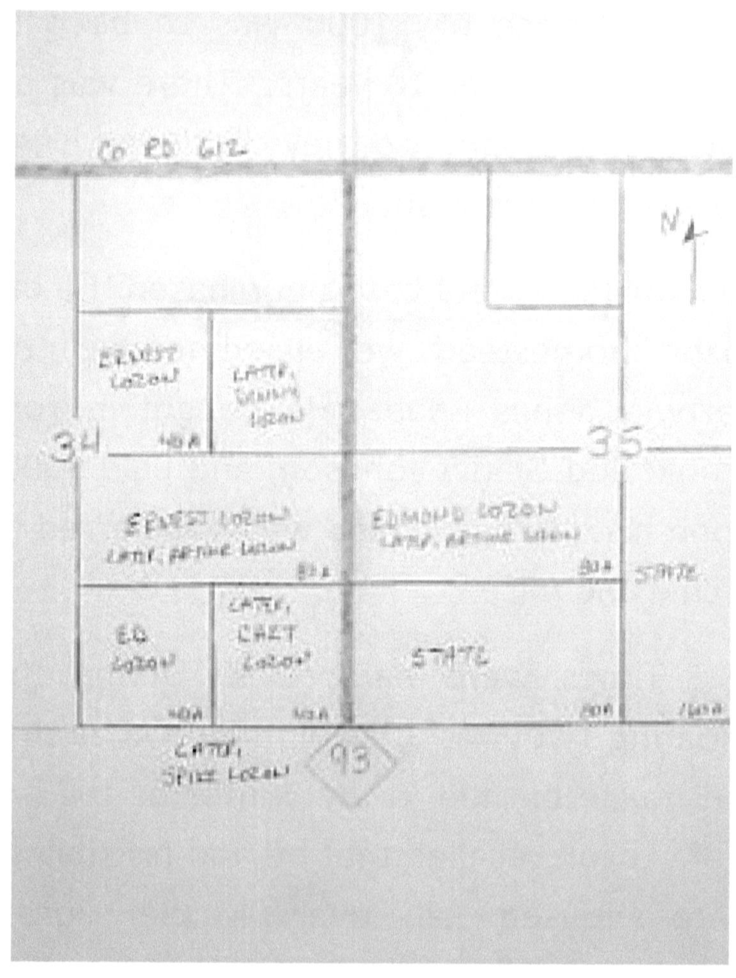

The preceding page shows a plat map of our area of Maple Forest Township, 1957 or 1958. Chet bought his acreage in 1959, and Spike bought land adjacent south of Chet's (area not on map).

Archie was supposed to pay $100 per year on the Goblet land, but it wasn't paid off until 1935. Many years only the interest was paid. It took a full 10 extra years to pay off the debt. The Johnson land was finally paid off in 1931, when Paul's estate was settled.

Alice died in July 1944. (There is speculation in the family that she may have been diabetic.) When Ernie came home from World War II, he and Doris married, and moved into the house with Archie, Ona, and Phyllis. Ona got married the same month, only to divorce the next year. Phyllis left and was married the following spring. Archie sold the farm to Ernie and Doris in 1946. They purchased an additional 80 acres from Arthur Howse in 1953.

The northern end of Hartwick Pines Road was pretty well covered with Lozons between 1940 and 1980.

Gradually all the places in Maple Forest were sold, but Grayling will always feel like home for much of the family.

Back – front, L – R: Dale, Gwen, Dick, Art, Emma, Jack, Evelyn, and Chet 1968

Everybody got married and had babies. Ed married three times; Ina Turner, Marie Tracy, and finally Pauline Johnson. Ona was only married a short time. Bob married Anna Cotter, and Chet married Evelyn Jordan. Ernie married Doris Castle, and Clyde (Spike) married Patricia McColman. Phyllis married Thomas Manier, and moved to California. Archie died in 1968 of a cerebral embolism.

Chester & Evelyn Lozon

50th Anniversary—May 4, 1983

L – R: Ellie, Evvie holding Marty, Jim on Art's shoulders, Chet with Denny, Dale, Gwen, Dick behind Emma, Donna, and Jack holding Mike. 1959

And they all lived happily ever after!

****

This is the end of my story. I hope you passed a pleasant hour or two reading our little book.

This didn't start out as my project—Doris Lozon spent 16 years (on and off) compiling the nine pounds of supporting documents for this book. Ancestry research is long and painful, with many letters written, phone calls made, cemeteries walked, and family Bibles searched. All of this was compounded by the various spellings of names, and the frequent recycling of names through several generations. Not to mention that folks seldom kept track of their children's birthdates. Many times, the only record of a birth within a family is the sudden appearance of 6 or 8 children between censuses. Often, several children in the same family were named Marie. And add in the fact that most of the records were in French, and you can begin to understand the monumental task she undertook for all of us!

It seemed a shame that she had gone to all that effort for naught, so I picked up where she left off, and finished the project. I feel it is important to have this information out there, just in case one person in the future wants to look back, and see what our pioneer ancestors were like.

I will place copies of this book, if possible, in the libraries of Grayling, Bay City, Montreal, Sault Ste. Marie, and University of Michigan.

Every word in this book is true, according to the papers in my possession. I have all the proof papers for this book at my home. Anybody who is interested is more than welcome to wade through it all! Information about ordering additional copies of this book can be obtained at thedinosaurlady@yahoo.com.

The generations have continued, of course, but they aren't my stories to tell. Maybe someone a few generations down the line will read this, and be interested in writing Volume 2: Jacques and Gilles in the New World. If so, I have compiled quite a bit of information on the folks between Chet & Evvie's children and my generation's grandchildren.

Map of the Generations

1. **Gilles Lauzon** (1631-1687) married **Marie Archambault** (1644-1685) *** Michelle, Marguerite, Francoise, Marie, Catherine, Seraphin, Louise, **Michel**, Paul, Marie Madeleine, Anne, and Jeanne.

2. **Michel Lauzon** (1673-1749) married **Marie-Anne Coitou** (1673-1749) *** Francois-Marie, Michael, Madeleine, Marie-Joseph, Marie-Raphael, Marie-Anne, Pierre, Catherine, and **Gabriel**.

3. **Gabriel Lauzon** (1715-?) married **Marie-Anne LaCombe** (1727-?) *** Marie Anne, Marie-Joseph, Marie

Catherine, Pierre-Gabriel, **Joseph Amable**, and Marie-Genevieve.

4. **Joseph Amable Lauzon** (1756-?) married **Marie Libersan** (CA 1756/60-?) *** Antoine, Josephte, and **Michel**.

5. **Michel Lauzon** (1784-?) married **Marguerite Chauret** (1784-?) *** Augustin, Felix, Isaac, Francis Xavier, **Isadore**, Adalaide, Marguerite, Marie, and Esther.

6. **Isadore Lauzon** (1811-1860) married **Pelagie Usereau** (1819-1909) *** Denise, Louise-Arvide, Amedee, Isadore Jr, Domitilde, John Baptiste,

Marguerite, Marcelle, **Napolean (Paul),** Arvide, Aglae, and William.

7. **Paul Lozon** (1852-1928) married **Mary Dore** (1855-1920) *** Josephime, **Archie**, Mary Louise, Joseph, Telesphore, Oddelia, and Laura.

8. **Archie Lozon** (1883-1968) married **Alice Traxler** (1885-1944) *** Edmund, Ona, Robert, **Chester**, Ernest, Clyde (Spike), and Phyllis.

9. **Chester Lozon** (1910-1984) married **Evelyn Jordan** (1914-2006) ***

   John Henry (Jack), Arthur Jerome (Art), Richard (Dick), Emma, Gwen, and Ernest Dale (Dale).

CHART 1

Lauzon/Coitou

Michel Lauzon
b. 19 Feb 1673
PtTrmbls, Qbc.
m. 15 May 1702
PtTrmbls, Qbc.
d. 8 Nov 1749
StGnvv, Mtl, Qbc

Marie-Anne Coitou
b. 12 Feb 1687
Cntrcr, Qbc.
d. 22 May 1726
RvrPrrs, Qbc.

Gilles Lauzon
b. 1631
StJLN,CAEN,NMDY
m. 27 Nov 1656
Montreal, Qbc.
d. 21 Sep 1687
Montreal, Qbc.

Marie Archambault
b. 1644
Dompierre, Aunnis
d. 8 Aug 1685, Mtr

Jean Coitou/StJean
b. 1648 Brtny, FR
m. Jul 1676
Cntrcr, Qbc.
d. 9 Nov 1726
PtTrmbls, Qbc.

Marie-Therese Petit
b. 1652, Paris, FR
d.
KING'S DAUGHTER

Pierre Lauzon
b. 1600
d.

Anne Boivin
b. 1604
d. 27 Nov 1656

Jacques Archambault
b. 1604 *Co. of 100 Assoc.*
d. 15 Feb 1688

Francoise Tourneau
b. 1600
d. 9 Dec 1663

Pierre Coitou
b.
d. NNTS,BRTGN,FR.

b.
d.

Pierre Petit
b.
d. ST.ETN-D-GRS,FR.

Marguerite Blondeau
b.
d. ST.ETN-D-GRS,FR.

Continued
On Chart 3

CHART 2

LaCombe/
Diel

Etienne LaCombe
b.
d. ST.SNCTR,FR.

Jean LaCombe I
b. 1648
m. 20 Jun 1678, Mtr.
SHIPPED W/ GILLES

Marguerite LeRoux
b.
d. ST.SNCTR,FR.

Marie-Charlotte Millet
b. 25 Nov 1662
d. 17 Mar 1751
PtTrmbls, Qbc.

Nicolas Millet
b. 1632
d. 9 Mar 1674
SHIPPED W/ GILLES

Jean LaCombe II
b. 25 Jan 1683
PtTrmbls, Qbc
m.
d.

Catherine Lorion
b. 1636
d. 20 Apr 1720

Marguerite Diel
b. 14 Jun 1691
LaPrre, Qbc.
d.

Phillip Diel/LaPetit
b.
d. ST.CLMBN,FR.

Charles Diel/LaPetit
b. 1652 Rouen, FR.
m. 31 Aug 1676, MNTRL
d.

Marie Hanquetin
b.
d. ST.CLMBN,FR.

Marie-Anne Picard
b. 3 Nov 1663, MNTRL
d. 4 Feb 1697, MNTRL

Jacques-Hughes Picard
b. Abt 1627
d. 22 Dec 1707

Antoinette DeLiercourt
b.1604-1630
d. 30 Sep 1707

Continued
On Chart 3

CHART 3

Lauzon/Libersan

Joseph Amable Lauzon
b. 23 Mar 1756
PFNDS, StGNVV, MNTRL
m. 31 Jan 1780
St Gnvv, Mntrl, Qbc
d.
SP: Marie Libersan

See Chart 9

Continued On Chart 4

Gabriel Lauzon
b. 27 Mar 1715
RvrPrre, Qbc.
m. 15 Jan 1746
SltRclt, Qbc.
d. 20 Aug 1776
StGNVV, MNTRL,Qbc.

Marie-Anne LaCombe
b. 8 May 1727
RvrPrre, Qbc.
d.

Michel Lauzon
b. 19 Feb 1673
PtTrmbls, Qbc.
m. 15 May 1702
PtTrmbls, Qbc.
d. 8 Nov 1749
StGnvv, Mtl, Qbc

Marie-Anne Coitou
b. 12 Feb 1687
Cntrcr, Qbc.
d. 22 May 1726
RvrPrrs, Qbc.

Jean LaCombe II
b. 25 Jan 1683
PtTrmbls, Qbc
m.
d.

Marguerite Diel
b. 14 Jun 1691
LaPrre, Qbc.
d.

CHART 4

Lauzon/Usereau

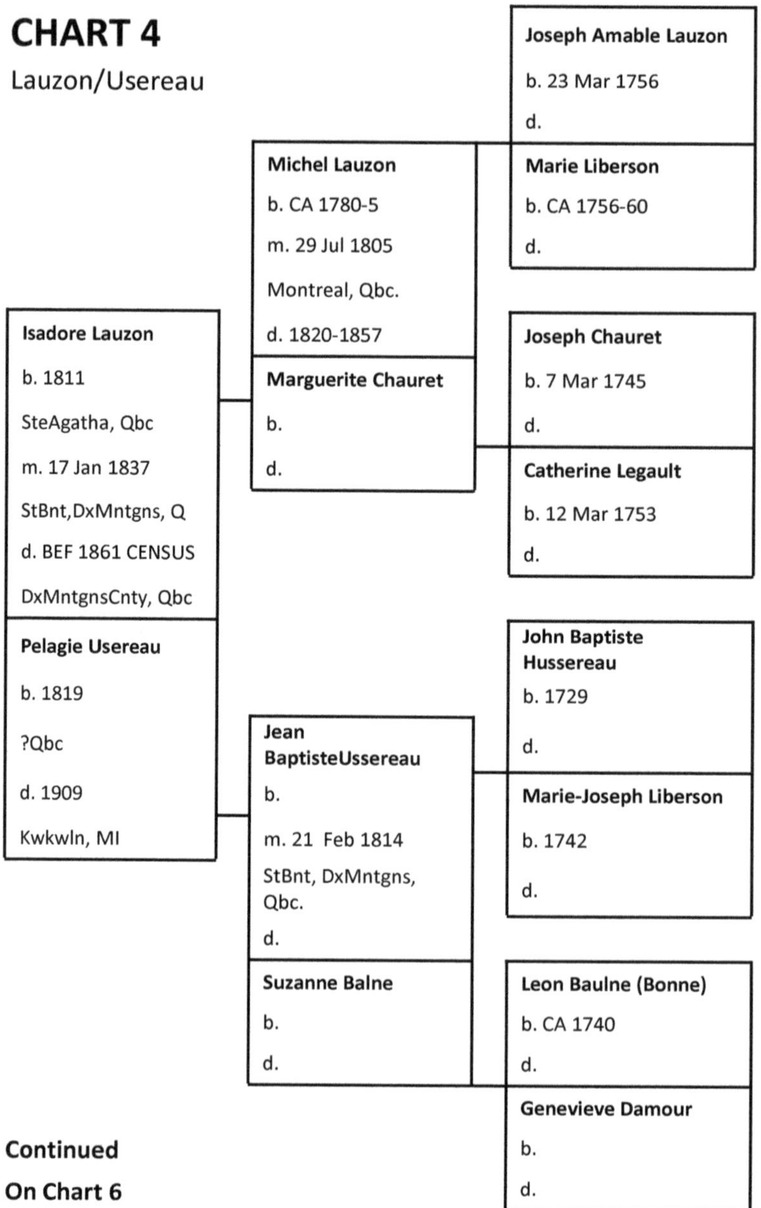

Continued

On Chart 6

CHART 5

Dore/Bissonnet

Gabriel Dore
b. Cir 1819
?Qbc
m. 30 Oct 1843
StPlycrp, Slngs, Qbc.
d. Dec 1883
Kwkwln, MI

Adele Bissonnet
b. 4 Jan 1825
?Mntrl, Qbc
d, 10 Sep 1914
Esxvl, By, MI

Antoine Dore
b. 17 Dec 1793
m. 14 Sep 1812
d.

Ursule Aumais
b.
d. 1833
StPoly, MNTRL, Qbc.

Germain Bissonnet
b. 25 Jul 1768
m. 15 Aug 1814
d.

Genevieve Ranger
b.
d.

Antoine Dore
b. 28 Feb 1764
d.

Josephte Cedilot
b. 1771
d.

Jean-Baptiste Aumais
b.
d.

Ursule Ranger
b.
d.

Germain Bissonnet
b. 25 Jul 1768
d.

Therese Monpetit
b. 5 Feb 1760
d.

Michael Ranger
b. CA 1765
d.

Marie Parent/Parant
b.
d.

Continued
On Chart 6

CHART 6

Lozon/Traxler

Archie Lozon
b. 3 Jul 1883
Kwkwln, By, MI
m. 8 Feb 1904
Kwkwln, By, MI
d. 28 Feb 1968
Glrd, Otsg, MI
Sp: Alice Traxler

See Chart 12

Paul (Napolean) Lozon
b. Feb 1852
DxMntgnCnty, Qbc
m. CA 1879
Kwkwln, BY, MI
d. 26 Jun 1928
ByCty, By, MI

Mary Dore
b. Oct 1855
StPlycrp, Slngs, Qbc.
d. 22 Jan 1920
ByCty, By, MI

Isadore Lauzon
b. 1811
SteAgatha, Qbc
m. 17 Jan 1837
StBnt,DxMntgns, Q
d. BEF 1861 CENSUS
DxMntgnsCnty, Qbc

Pelagie Usereau
b. 1819
?Qbc
d. 1909
Kwkwln, MI

Gabriel Dore
b. Cir 1819
?Qbc
m. 30 Oct 1843
StPlycrp, Slngs, Qbc.
d. Dec 1883
Kwkwln, MI

Adele Bissonnet
b. 4 Jan 1825
?Mntrl, Qbc
d, 10 Sep 1914
Esxvl, By, MI

CHART 7

Libersan/Devoyau

Antoine Liberson
b. 28 Oct 1704
Mntrl, Qbc.
m. 9 Jul 1731
StLrnt, Mntrl, Qbc

M.Jeanne Devoyau
b. 21 Jan 1715
Mntrl, Qbc.
d.

Leonard Liberson
b. 1671,
RAZA,PRGRD,FR
m. 23 Jul 1703
StLrnt, Mntrl, Qbc
d. 30 Nov 1751
StLrnt, Mntrl, Qbc

Jeanne Beaudry
b. 8 Sep 1674
Mntrl, Qbc
d. 19 Mar 1756
StLrnt, Mntrl, Qbc

Pierre Devoyau
b. CA1682
m. 24 May 1706, Mntrl
d. 11 Oct 1758
StLrnt, Mntrl, Qbc

M. Jean Prevost
b. 13 Jan 1687, Qbc
d. 24 Feb 1755
StLrnt, Mntrl, Qbc

Guillaume Liberson
b.
d. RAZA,PRGRD,FR

Marie-Madeleine Liberson
b.
d. RAZA,PRGRD,FR

Antoine Beaudry/L'epinette
b.
d. *SHIPPED W/ GILLES*

Catherine Guyard
b. 1639, PARIS,FR.
d. 1703 *KING'S DAUGHTER*

Leonard Devoyau
b. MASTER WEAVER
d. POITIU,FR.

Anne Letay
b.
d.

Jean Provost
b. CA 1653
d. 24 May 1706

Francoise LeBlanc
b. 19 Jan 1623
d.

Continued
On Chart 9

CHART 8

Dumay/Lanthier

Francois Dumay/Demers
b. 5 Mar 1712
Mntrl, Qbc.
m. 1731
Montreal?
d.

Anne Lanthier
b. 24 Oct 1709
Blvu, Qbc.
d. 9 May 1749
StGnvv, Mntrl, Qbc.

Robert Dumay/Demers
b. 11 Jan 1671
Varennes, Qbc
m. 26 Apr 1694
Mntrl, Qbc
d. 23 May 1741
Mntrl, Qbc

Madeleine Jette
b. 16 Dec 1673
d. 10 Jul 1737

Jacques Lanthier
b.
Poitou, FR
d. 8 Feb 1694
Mntrl, Qbc.

Catherine-Angelique Matou
b. 14 May 1672
Quebec City, Quebec
d. 1711

Andre Demers/Dumets
b. 3 Feb 1623
d. 17 Jul 1711

Marie Chefdeville
b. 1636
d. 23 Nov 1708

Urbain Jette
b. 1627 *SHIPPED W/ GILLES*
d. 13 May 1684

Catherine Charles
b. 1638
d. 26 Jan 1659

b.
d.

b.
d.

Phillipe Matou
b. 1635
d. 20 Jan 1688

Marguerite Doucinet
b. 1643
d.

Continued On Chart 9

CHART 9

Lauzon/Libersan

Marie Libersan
b. CA 1757-60
m. 31 Jan 1780
StGnvv, Mntrl, Qbc
d.
SP: Joseph Amable Lauzon

See Chart 3

Francis Libersan
b. 1734
StLrnt, Mntrl, Qbc
m. 3 May 1757
StGnvv, Mntrl, Qbc
d.

Angelique Dumay/Demers
b. CA 1738
Quebec
d.

Antoine Liberson
b. 28 Oct 1704
Mntrl, Qbc.
m. 9 Jul 1731
StLrnt, Mntrl, Qbc

M.Jeanne Devoyau
b. 21 Jan 1715
Mntrl, Qbc.
d.

Francois Dumay/Demers
b. 5 Mar 1712
Mntrl, Qbc.
m. 1731
Montreal?
d.

Anne Lanthier
b. 24 Oct 1709
Blvu, Qbc.
d. 9 May 1749
StGnvv, Mntrl, Qbc.

Continued
On Chart 4

CHART 10

Traxler/McCubbin

John P Traxler
b. 8 Dec 1817
KntCty, Ont.
m. 19 Jul 1837
KntCty, Ont.
d. 9 May 1883
Harwich, Kent, Ont.

Mary Ann McCubbin
b. Jun 1819
NwBrnswk
d. 3 Oct 1873
Kent Co, Ont.

Peter Traxler Jr
b. CA 1775-8
PA, USA
m. CA 1800
Kent Co, Ont.
d. 18 Jul 1846
Kent Co, Ont.

Rebecca Fields
b. CA 1780
near Niagra, Ont.
d. CA 1869

Robert McCubbin
b. 3 Oct 1783
Glwy, Sctld
m. CA 1803, Scotland
d. 3 Jun 1873
Chtm, Kent, Ont.

Mary Carson
b. 3 Jun 1788
Dmfrsre, Sctlnd
d. Apr, Chtm, Kent, Ont

Peter Traxler Sr
b. CA 1750
d. 12 Nov 1825

Barbara?
b.
d.

Nathan Fields
b.
d. 29 Aug 1809-1810

Amy Slack/Slaught
b. 22 Feb 1772
d. 6 Dec 1854

b.
d.

b.
d.

b.
d.

b.
d.

Continued
On Chart 12

CHART 11

Winter/Zavitz

Henry Winter
b. CA 1741
d.

b.
d.

Peter Winter
b. CA 1767
PA, USA
m.
d.

Henry Winter
b. 1798
m. 1822, Eloped
d. 4 May 1876
Kent Co, Ont.

Catherine?
b. PA, USA
d.

b.
d.

b.
d.

Rebecca Zavitz
b. 1802
BertieTwp,Wllnd, Ont
d. 5 Oct 1887
DvrTwp,KentCo,Ont.

Jacob Zavitz
b. Aug 1752
CntrVly, NHmptn, PA
m. 1780, Tnrsvl, PA
d. 12 Jan 1815
Ontario

b.
d.

b.
d.

Cadarina Learn
b. 25 Jun 1760
Nrthmptn, PA
d. 9 Oct 1856
Wlnd, Wnflt, Ont.

b.
d.

b.
d.

Continued
On Chart 12

CHART 12

Lozon/Traxler

John P Traxler
b. 8 Dec 1817
KntCty, Ont.
m. 19 Jul 1837
KntCty, Ont.
d. 9 May 1883
Harwich, Kent, Ont.

Robert Traxler
b. 12 May 1844
KntCnty,Cnty, Ont.
m. 1867
KntCnty,Cnty, Ont.
d. 16 Oct 1916
Kwkwln,By,MI

Mary Ann McCubbin
b. Jun 1819
NwBrnswk
d. 3 Oct 1873
Kent Co, Ont.

Alice Traxler
b. 16 Sep 1885
? Michigan
m. 8 Feb 1904
Kwkwln,By,MI
d. 18 Jul 1944
Grlng,Crfrd, MI
SP: Archie Lozon

See Chart 6

Margaret Winter
b. 11 May 1848
KntCnty, Ont
d. 1 Oct 1925
Kwkwln,By,MI

Henry Winter
b. 1798
m. 1822, Eloped
d. 4 May 1876
Kent Co, Ont.

Rebecca Zavitz
b. 1802
BertieTwp,Wllnd, Ont
d. 5 Oct 1887
DvrTwp,KentCo,Ont.

Sources of Information

A. PUBLIC

1. Church Records -- Miscellaneous.

2. Church Records -- St. Benoit Catholic Church; deux Montagnes County, Quebec.

3. Church Record -- St. Polycarpe Catholic Church; Soulanges County, Quebec.

4. Ontario Census – 1851, 1871.

5. Quebec Census – 851, 1871.

6. U.S. Census.

7. Vital Records -- Michigan.

B. PRIVATE

1. Feldhauser, Bernard: Private papers.

2. Highly, Dahn: Private papers.

3. McCubbin Family Bible; owned by Doris Keil: Kent County, Ontario.

C. MICROFILMED

1. Fabian Marriage Index.

2. Loiselle Marriage Index.

D. PUBLISHED

1. Cemetery Transcriptions. Traxler Cemetery, River Thames; Kent County Branch, Ontario Genealogical Society.

2. Candage, Charles Samuel and Peak, Ralph Ernest. Heard-Hurd Genealogy 1610-1987. Camden, Maine: Picton Press

3. Clark, Helen Annett Zavitz. Benjamin and Esther Augustine; Their Ancestors and Descendants. Self-pub.

4. Commemorative Biographical Record. Kent County, Ontario.

5. Crysler, Ethel. Partial WINTER Family Genealogy (chart III K pp. 1-15). Compiled by Robert E. Zavitz, Wallaceburg, Ontario: 1964

6. Drouin, Gabriel. Dictionnaire National des Canadiens Francais (1608-1760). Montreal: Institut Genealogique Drouin, 1965: rev. Ed.

7. Jette, Rene. Dictionaire Genealogique des Familles du Quebec, des Origins a 1730. Montreal: Les presses de 'l Universite de Montreal. 1983.

8. LaForest, Thomas J. Our French-Canadian Ancestors. Palm Harbor, Florida: Lisi Press, 1983.

9. LeBoef, J. Arthur. Complement au Dictionnaire Genealogique Tanguay. 2 Volumes in 1; Montreal: Canadien-Francaise. 1977.

10. Olivier, Reginald L. Your Ancient Canadian Family Ties. Logan, Utah. Everton Publishers, Inc.; 1972.

11. Pierce, Franklin Clifton. Field Genealogy. Chicago: Hammond Press, W.B. Conklin Co. 1901.

12. Reisinger, Joy and Courteau, Elmer. The King's Daughters. Sparta, Wisconsin: Joy Reisinger.

13. Tanguay, Cyprien. Dictionnaire Genealogique des Familles Canadiens; 7 Volumes. Montreal: Eusabe Senecal, 1871-1890; reprinted, Montreal: Editions Elysee, 1975 and Pawtucket, R.I. 1982. Quintin-Rock Pubs.

E. INTERNET

1. "Gilles Lauzon". *Wikipedia*. http://en.m.wikipedia.org/wiki/Gilles_Lauzon. 1 Nov 2013.

2. "History of Canada". *Wikipedia*. http://en.m.wikipedia.org/wiki/Canada%2C_history_of. 13 Nov 2013.

3. History of the Montreal Prison from A.D. 1784 to A.D. 1886. http://archive.org/stream/cihm_00186/cihm_00186_djvu.txt. 4 Nov 2013.

4. "Jacques Archambault". *Wikipedia*. http://en.m.wikipedia.org/wiki/Jacques_Archambault. 6 Nov 2013.

5. "Les Descendants de Sebastien Cholet – marriage avec Ann Heard". www.genealogie.org/famille/cholette/emain0002.html. 2 Jan 2014.

6. "New France 1650-1654". http://metis-history.info/french15.shtml. 7 Nov 2013.

7. "Rootsweb WorldConnect Project: Jack and Bonnie Cholette's Family Tree".

http://wc.rootsweb.ancestry.com/cgi-bin/igm. 2 Jan 2014

8. "Timeline of Montreal History". *Wikipedia*. http://en.m.wikipedia.org/wiki/Timeline_of_Montreal_history. 7 Nov 2013.

www.ingramcontent.com/pod-product-compliance
Ingram Content Group UK Ltd.
Pitfield, Milton Keynes, MK11 3LW, UK
UKHW040559210726
13854UKWH00008B/1500

9 781304 621429